And Justice for All

Gail Blasser Riley

STECK-VAUGHN
ELEMENTARY · SECONDARY · ADULT · LIBRARY

A Harcourt Company

www.steck-vaughn.com

Photography: p.5 ©K.G. Murti/Visuals Unlimited, Inc.; p.10 ©Mark Burnett/Stock Boston, Inc./PictureQuest; p.12 ©Geo Musil/Visuals Unlimited, Inc.; p.15 ©Scott Barrow/International Stock; pp.17, 24 ©Bettmann/ CORBIS; p.31 ©SuperStock, Inc.; p.40 ©Bob Daemmrich/ Stock Boston, Inc./PictureQuest; p.47 ©Mark E. Gibson/ Visuals Unlimited, Inc.; p.49 ©Joe Atlas/Artville; p.50 ©Rafael Macia/Photo Researchers, Inc.; p.55 ©Joseph Sohm/Visions of America, LLC/PictureQuest.

Additional photography by CORBIS, MetaTools, and PhotoDisc, Inc.

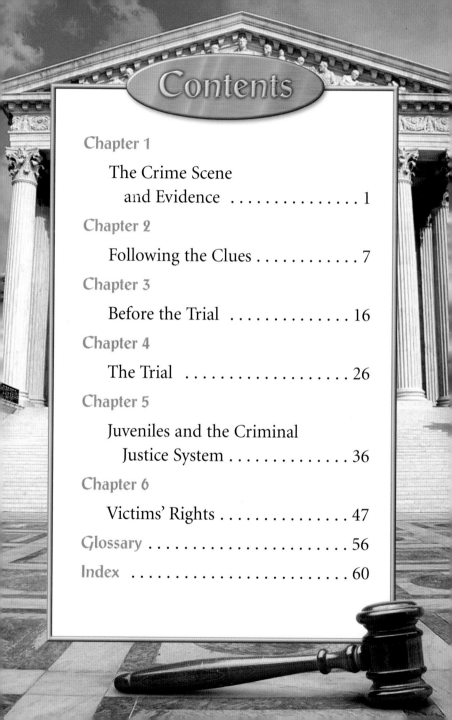

Contents

CHAPTER 1

The Crime Scene and Evidence

A murder victim is discovered. The police search the crime scene for tiny scraps of evidence. They piece them all together and arrest a suspect. Is the **accused** guilty of the crime?

In the early 1980s, Kenneth Waters was charged with a murder. His sister, Betty Anne Waters, was sure that Kenneth was innocent.

Kenneth was **tried** in a Massachusetts court. At the trial, the lawyer for the state attempted to prove that Kenneth was guilty. The lawyer for the state also is called the **prosecuting lawyer.**

◄ *Criminal cases are often tried in courtrooms like this one.*

The defense lawyer presented Kenneth's side of the story. He said that Kenneth had an alibi and couldn't have **committed** the murder. He had been somewhere else when the murder happened.

As Betty Anne sat in court and listened to the lawyers, so did the **jury**. The members of the jury listened carefully to all the evidence presented during the trial. Then they voted on whether Kenneth was guilty or not guilty. To **convict** Kenneth, members of the jury had to believe that he was guilty.

After they heard the evidence, the jury decided on a **verdict** of guilty. Betty Anne was horrified. She watched as her brother was taken away to spend the rest of his life in prison.

This trial was not Kenneth's last chance to show that he was not guilty. When a trial is over, the **defendant** can appeal a guilty verdict in an appeals court. This court hears the case again to decide whether the verdict should change or stay the same. ⚡

Kenneth appealed the verdict. Betty Anne was sure that he would be freed. She was wrong. The verdict didn't change.

Betty Anne was sure that her brother wasn't the killer. She didn't know how to help him, though. She was raising two children and couldn't afford to pay more lawyers.

A Do-It-Yourself Approach

Betty Anne decided that she would study to become a lawyer. Then she could fight to free her brother. It would be a difficult task because Betty Anne hadn't even finished high school. She had to go to school, work, and take care of her children.

First, she finished high school. Then, she took college classes. Betty Anne finally entered law school in 1995. By then, Kenneth already had served 12 years in prison.

In law school, Betty Anne learned about evidence. For hundreds of years, juries mostly heard accounts from witnesses and from officers who investigated crimes. More recently, police had begun using fingerprints as evidence. Each human being has fingerprints unlike those of any other person. Fingerprints can help show whether the accused was at the crime scene.

The newest kind of evidence interested Betty Anne most. This evidence was based on DNA, a chemical pattern that occurs in every cell of the body. A person's DNA is the same whether it is in hair, **saliva**, blood, tissue, or other body parts. Like fingerprints, no two people's DNA is exactly alike. Police sometimes find bits of hair, saliva, or blood at a crime scene. These clues can be very important.

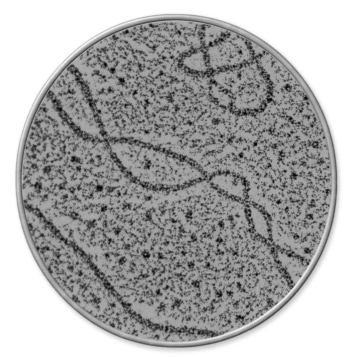

A strand of DNA can prove someone guilty or innocent.

No one had used DNA evidence in Kenneth's trial. Betty Anne wondered if this type of evidence might prove he was innocent.

What DNA Proved

In 1998, after Betty Anne became an attorney, she spent most of her time working on her brother's case. She took cases for some friends, but she had no other **clients**.

To help her brother, Betty Anne knew that she needed evidence from the crime scene. Did the evidence still exist? Massachusetts law said that evidence could be thrown away ten years after all appeals were completed. More than ten years had passed since Kenneth's appeals.

Betty Anne kept asking a courthouse worker to look for any evidence that still might be stored somewhere. Finally, the worker found a box of evidence in the courthouse basement. The box held bloody items that had been found at the crime scene.

A DNA test proved that Kenneth's blood didn't match the criminal's blood found at the crime scene. Betty Anne shared this information and other new evidence with a group of lawyers. This group of lawyers helped prisoners like Kenneth use new DNA evidence to challenge verdicts. After nearly twenty years in prison, Kenneth was freed.

CHAPTER 2

Following the Clues

Many clues, such as fingerprints or DNA, can be difficult to find. Some clues, however, are very obvious to police officers at a crime scene.

In Kentucky, two men decided to rob an automatic **teller** machine (ATM). They thought it would be full of thousands of dollars and that it would easily pop open. They planned to wrap a heavy chain around the front of the ATM and use their truck to rip the cover off.

The men tossed the chain into the back of their pickup truck and headed for an ATM. Once there, they hooked one end of the chain to the truck's back **bumper**. They wrapped the other end of the chain around the front cover of the ATM. One of the men jumped in the truck and stepped on the gas pedal. The other man waited to pick up the stacks of money. ⚡

You might have guessed what happened next. The little ATM machine was much stronger than it looked. The front of the machine did not pop off. Instead, the back bumper tore away from the truck. Afraid of getting caught, the crooks sped away. They left the bumper behind.

When police officers got there, they found some important evidence still attached to the bumper—the truck's license plate! The police used it to track down the criminals.

This isn't the only case in which criminals have left easy clues. Some robbers have left their **wallets** at crime scenes, with driver's licenses inside! Others have hurt themselves while committing a crime and called 911 for help.

Everyone Leaves a Clue

What about clues that are harder to find and understand? Detectives are skilled in finding clues such as fingerprints. A fingerprint that's been left in something like blood or ink can be easy to find. Otherwise, prints are very difficult or even impossible to see at first glance. However, that doesn't mean they aren't there.

When a person touches a surface, that person leaves behind oils from his or her skin. The oil forms a fingerprint. To find such prints, detectives brush special powder across surfaces found at the crime scene. This powder sticks to the oils, making the fingerprints easier to see. Detectives use special tapes or glues to "lift" the prints off the surface and preserve them.

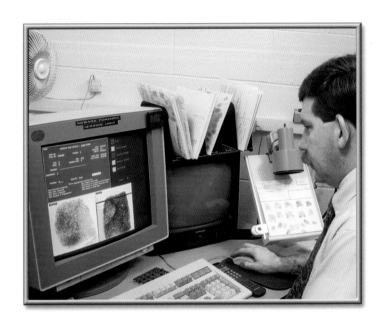

Computers have made it easier to compare records of fingerprints.

Detectives use computers to check lifted prints against records from around the world. In this way, they might be able to match the fingerprints to the person who made them.

At a crime scene, detectives might also collect samples of hair, skin, blood, and bones. All of these materials contain DNA. Scientists test the DNA to find out if it matches the DNA of any known criminals. Like fingerprints, DNA records are stored on computers. Many times there is no matching record at the time of the search. In such cases a match might be found later after arrests are made for other crimes.

Caught!

Fingerprints and DNA evidence have led to arrests in many older cases that had not been solved. In the year 2000, DNA evidence helped close two murder cases that police had been working on for years.

The murders happened three months apart in 1996 in Arlington, Texas. The crimes were very similar. Both victims were young women. Officers thought that one person had committed both of the murders.

At each crime scene, officers found fingerprints and DNA material. The officers entered the fingerprints into computers. They found no match, but the fingerprints stayed in the computers. That way, the prints could be matched against any prints collected in the future.

Officers worked hard to solve the cases. Then, finally, they had a break. Four years after the murders, they found a fingerprint at a **burglary** scene. They arrested a suspect and took his fingerprints. Officers entered the fingerprints from the burglary scene into computers. They found that those fingerprints also matched those found at both murder scenes four years earlier.

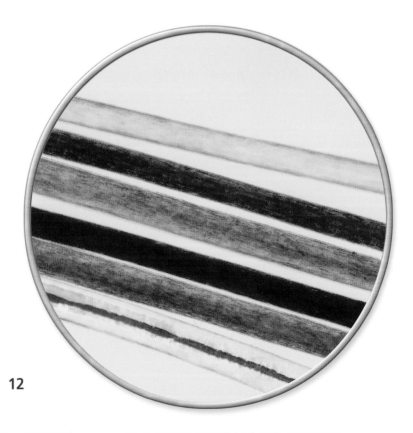

Officers hadn't realized the importance at the time, but they had questioned this man just after the first murder. They had talked to him only because he had lived in the same apartment building as the victim. They had not fingerprinted him or other residents of the building. The fingerprints from the burglary scene gave police the evidence they needed. They linked the man to the 1996 murders.

Other Clues

Detectives also search crime scenes for weapons or bullets. They look for tools the criminal used to enter a crime scene. If a criminal smashed a window, detectives can put together the pieces of glass from the broken window. They might later find a tiny piece of window glass in a suspect's home or car. This tiny piece of evidence can complete the "window puzzle." Even threads from clothing can be used as clues.

◀ *Police use microscopes to compare strands of hair.*

Detectives might find tire tracks and shoe prints at a crime scene. This is known as **imprint** evidence. These tracks and prints are carefully photographed. They later can be compared to a suspect's car or shoes.

Tire tracks are photographed from above. At least one photo of the whole tire track is taken. Detectives often also take close-up photos of small parts of the tire track. Different types of tires leave different kinds of tracks. Therefore, tire tracks can tell something about the car or truck the suspect was driving.

Detectives photograph shoe prints alone and in groups. The pictures show how each shoe print looks. They also show the criminal's stride, or the distance between steps. When they photograph shoe prints, police photographers place a light at the side of the print. The light and shadows help show details.

In addition to taking photographs, detectives often film crime scenes. Photographs and films might be used later as evidence before and during the trial.

Police officers have to be very careful about how they collect and test evidence. They also have to be careful about the conclusions they draw. At the trial, the defendant's lawyer will ask the police lots of questions about the evidence.

Shoes and tires can leave important clues behind.

CHAPTER 3

Before the Trial

"You have the right to remain silent. Anything you say can and will be held against you in a court of law."

You might have heard this warning many times in movies or on television. Police officers really do say these words, or something very similar, during an arrest.

A Cold Chicago Morning

This warning has its roots in two court cases. The first was an arrest made in early 1960. Chicago police were looking for a killer. They suspected a man named Danny Escobedo.

One cold morning in January, police picked up Escobedo and took him in for questioning. As the officers drove him to the station, they told

Danny Escobedo's case changed ▶ some rights for the accused.

Escobedo he should confess to the murder. They said a good friend of his had told them that Escobedo had fired the shots that killed the victim.

At the station, police put Escobedo in a small room. There they asked him questions and attempted to make him confess. Escobedo's lawyer came to the station. Escobedo and his lawyer kept asking to talk to one another, but they never were allowed to do so.

The police questioned Escobedo for a long time. Still, he stuck to his story. He told officers that he hadn't shot anyone.

After many hours, officers brought in Escobedo's "friend." This was the man who said Escobedo had done the shooting. Escobedo looked at him and cried out, "I didn't shoot Manuel. You did it!"

Later, because he was tired after all the questioning, Escobedo signed a **confession**. He said he had hired the friend to do the murder.

During the trial, Escobedo said that he had been tricked by the police. Though he denied his confession, the jury found him guilty. Escobedo decided to appeal the verdict.

The U. S. Constitution gives Americans, such as Danny Escobedo, rights and freedoms.

You Have the Right to an Attorney

Escobedo's case eventually came before the United States Supreme Court. This court does not review many cases like Escobedo's. To be heard in the Supreme Court, a case must raise an important issue.

In Danny Escobedo's case, the big issue was whether his lawyer should have been present while Escobedo was questioned. ⚡

Protected Rights

The Supreme Court bases its decisions on the U. S. Constitution, the set of basic laws of the United States. The Constitution was written in 1787, but it has been changed from time to time to include new ideas. Changes or additions to the Constitution are called **amendments.** These amendments **guarantee** Americans certain rights and freedoms.

The Sixth Amendment gives citizens the right to have a lawyer present during a criminal trial. When Danny Escobedo appealed his murder

conviction in the 1960s, the Supreme Court decided that the Sixth Amendment meant even more. It meant that the accused had the right to have a lawyer present during police questioning.

The Court also said that the police had **violated** Escobedo's Fourteenth Amendment rights. That amendment guarantees the right to a fair trial.

You Have the Right to Remain Silent

In Arizona, also in the early 1960s, a young woman was kidnapped and attacked. She escaped, though, and the police set out to find the man who had kidnapped her.

They arrested a man named Ernesto Miranda. They placed him in a police **lineup**. To make a lineup, police place a suspect in a group of other people who have a similar appearance. Then, the police ask the victim of the crime to identify the criminal. In this lineup, police asked the victim to pick out the man who had kidnapped her. The woman told police what she thought.

After the lineup, Miranda asked, "How did I do?" The officers replied that he'd failed the test, but this wasn't exactly true. The victim had said only that Miranda looked similar to the man who had attacked her. She couldn't say for sure that he was the right man.

Officers questioned Miranda. He didn't ask for a lawyer. The officers didn't tell him he could have a lawyer present. Records don't show whether they told Miranda he had the right to remain silent.

The police brought the victim to the questioning room. They asked Miranda to speak, hoping the victim could identify his voice. "Is that the girl?" the officers asked him.

Miranda believed the victim had already identified him. He answered, "That's the girl." Miranda signed a confession form and wrote the details of the crime.

The form said that Miranda knew his rights when he made the confession. However, police officers really hadn't explained to Miranda what his rights were. When he went to trial, Miranda was found guilty.

Miranda appealed the verdict. His case went to the United States Supreme Court.

The Supreme Court decided that police officers had violated Miranda's rights so that they could get his confession. The court ordered a new trial. This time, they said, his confession couldn't be used as evidence. In the new trial, the jury found Miranda guilty based on other evidence.

The Supreme Court made another ruling because of this case. They said that as soon as a suspect was arrested, he or she must be told about the right to remain silent. Suspects also must be told that their words can be used against them in court.

Today, most police officers carry a warning card to read aloud when they arrest someone. The Supreme Court didn't set down any exact wording. Each police department can choose its own wording.

Many years after the Supreme Court ruling on his case, Ernesto Miranda was killed in a fight. When police officers arrested a suspect in Miranda's murder, what did they tell him? "You have the right to remain silent."

Many police officers carry cards like this one that state a suspect's rights.

DEFENDANT

LOCATION

SPECIFIC WARNING REGARDING INTERROGATIONS

1. You have the right to remain silent.

2. Anything you say can and will be used against you in a court of law.

3. You have the right to talk to a lawyer and have him present with you while you are being questioned.

4. If you cannot afford to hire a lawyer one will be appointed to represent you before any questioning, if you wish one.

SIGNATURE OF DEFENDANT

DATE

TIME

WITNESS

☐ REFUSED SIGNATURE   SAN FRANCISCO POLICE DEPARTMENT

PR.9.1.4

More Rights for the Accused

The Fourth Amendment	protects suspects against **unreasonable** searches
The Fifth Amendment	states that the accused doesn't have to **testify** in his or her own criminal trial
The Sixth Amendment	states that the accused has a right to a lawyer, a right to a speedy public trial, and a right to question witnesses
The Eighth Amendment	• protects the accused against cruel and unusual punishment • gives the accused the right to post bail (This means that if the accused pays a certain amount of money, called bail, to the court, he or she does not have to stay in jail until the trial.)
The Fourteenth Amendment	gives the accused the right to a fair trial

CHAPTER 4

The Trial

In the United States, each state can make its own criminal laws. In the past, only some states gave people the right to have a lawyer during any criminal trial. If the accused couldn't afford a lawyer, the court provided one. Other states provided a lawyer only to people on trial for serious crimes. All of that changed when a man named Clarence Earl Gideon was arrested for a small crime.

In the 1960s, Gideon was accused of breaking into a Florida pool hall to steal some money. When police officers arrested him, Gideon said he couldn't afford to pay for a lawyer. He asked the judge to **appoint** one for him.

The judge refused. According to Florida law, the case was not serious enough.

The United States Supreme ▶
Court hears cases that raise
important issues.

Gideon had to act as his own lawyer. That's a lot to expect from someone who has had no training. A lawyer's role in a trial is very important. Without the help of a lawyer, an innocent person could be sent to prison.

How a Trial Works

At the beginning of a trial, the judge and the lawyers for both sides decide who will be on the jury. They question a number of people who might be chosen for the jury. Lawyers cannot pick the people they want. Instead, they can excuse the people they do not want on the jury. Experienced lawyers attempt to remove people whom they think can't be fair. That's important because the jury decides if the accused is guilty.

When the jury is in place, the lawyers give opening statements. The prosecuting lawyer describes how he or she will attempt to prove that the accused is guilty.

The defense lawyer states that the accused isn't guilty. This lawyer explains that it's up to the state to prove that the accused is guilty. The accused doesn't have to prove that he or she is innocent.

After opening statements, the case is tried by lawyers. The prosecuting lawyer begins by calling forth witnesses and asking them questions. This is called **direct examination**. This lawyer might ask eyewitnesses to tell what they saw or heard. He or she might ask police officers about evidence such as fingerprints.

The defense lawyer has a chance to ask these witnesses questions, too. This is called **cross-examination**. It gives the defense lawyer a chance to show that evidence might be faulty or that witnesses might not be truthful.

After the state's lawyer is finished, the defense lawyer has the right to call witnesses, too. However, he or she is not required to do so.

In addition to calling witnesses, lawyers can present exhibits to the jury. Exhibits can include photographs, weapons, or other evidence.

For the Defense

Defense lawyers can call witnesses who might help explain why the accused isn't guilty. What reasons might they give?

- *An alibi* A lawyer might argue that the accused was somewhere else when the crime happened, not at the crime scene. To prove the alibi, the lawyer must find witnesses who saw the accused at another place.

- *Self-defense* Did the accused hurt somebody only because he or she was defending himself or herself from being seriously injured or killed? It usually takes a skilled lawyer and strong witnesses to prove self-defense.

- *Insanity* This defense is rare. It doesn't mean that the accused didn't commit the crime. It means that the accused didn't know right from wrong or couldn't control his or her behavior because of a **mental** problem. This defense requires doctors who will speak about the mental health of the accused.

You might have heard news reports about a defendant who is not **competent** to stand trial. That's not the same thing as an insanity defense. If the accused is not competent to stand trial, it means he or she can't understand the charges and therefore can't help the lawyer put together a case.

Doctors might talk to a defendant to find out about the defendant's mental health.

If a defendant is not competent, he or she is sent to doctors for help. Later, if the defendant can understand the charges and help the lawyer, the case continues.

Wrapping Up the Case

When both sides have presented their case, the judge gives instructions to the members of the jury. The jury will use these instructions to help them decide on a verdict.

Next, the lawyers present their final arguments. These arguments can be very powerful. They are the last chance the lawyers have to persuade the jury.

Then, the jury goes to a private room where they carefully discuss the evidence and give their opinions. Finally, they take a vote to decide the verdict.

How Did Gideon Do?

You might remember that Clarence Earl Gideon served as his own lawyer in a Florida court. He did as well as he could for a person without legal training. He gave an opening statement to the jury. He questioned the witnesses who spoke against him. Gideon also presented a closing statement to the jury to argue against the charges. Still, the jury found Gideon guilty, and he was sentenced to five years in prison.

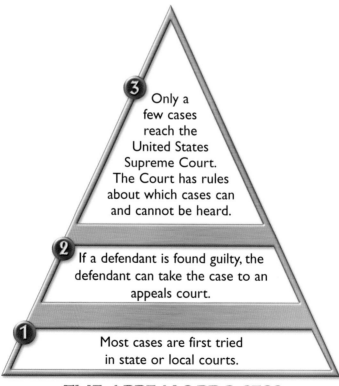

3 Only a few cases reach the United States Supreme Court. The Court has rules about which cases can and cannot be heard.

2 If a defendant is found guilty, the defendant can take the case to an appeals court.

1 Most cases are first tried in state or local courts.

THE APPEALS PROCESS

Gideon appealed the verdict. He argued that the verdict was unfair because he didn't have a real lawyer defending him. Finally, the court appointed a lawyer to handle his case. It rose through lower state courts and up to the United States Supreme Court.

How did the Supreme Court rule? How did it make its decision? The Supreme Court judges looked at an earlier case that was similar to Gideon's. That defendant had been unable to pay for a lawyer, and the judge had refused to appoint one. As a result, the defendant had been found guilty.

In Gideon's case, the Supreme Court ruled that Gideon had the right to a new trial with a lawyer to represent him. The judges based their decision on two amendments to the Constitution: the Sixth Amendment and the Fourteenth Amendment. The Sixth Amendment gives the accused the right to have a lawyer present. The Fourteenth Amendment guarantees the right to "due process," which means a fair trial for the accused. ⚡

After the Supreme Court made its decision, the case against Gideon was tried again in a Florida court. This time, the court appointed a lawyer for Gideon. The lawyer found new witnesses who showed that the state didn't have a strong case against Gideon. The jury's decision this time was *not guilty!*

Several years later, the Supreme Court heard another case about a defendant who hadn't had the money to pay a lawyer. The Court ruled that in *any* case in which the defendant could serve *any* time in jail or prison—even one day—the defendant had the right to a lawyer. The court would appoint a lawyer if the defendant could prove that he or she couldn't afford to pay an attorney.

CHAPTER 5

Juveniles and the Criminal Justice System

Juveniles commit many of the same types of crimes that adults do. Should they have the same rights as adults? Another real-life case made the Supreme Court think hard about that question.

In 1964, Gerald Gault was a 15-year-old boy who lived in Arizona. Though he was young, he already had been in trouble for stealing. He was assigned a **probation** officer.

One morning, Gerald and one of his friends got together and made an **improper** phone call to a neighbor. One of the boys used words that were very upsetting to the listener.

A phone call caused a lot of trouble for Gerald Gault.

The neighbor thought she recognized the voice of the caller, and she called the police. Gerald and his friend were arrested hours later. They were taken to a **detention home** for juveniles.

Gerald's father was out of town. When Gerald's mother arrived home from work and couldn't find Gerald, she asked his older brother to check the neighborhood. Only then did his family learn he had been arrested.

Gerald's mother and brother went to the detention home. There they met with the probation officer who'd handled Gerald's theft case. The officer explained that Gerald would have to stay in the detention home until the court hearing the following morning. The probation officer filed papers with the court to ask for a court hearing.

The papers didn't give the reason for Gerald's arrest. They only said that Gerald was in trouble because he'd violated his probation orders. The probation officer didn't give a copy of the papers to Gerald's family.

Gerald Admits Some Guilt

The next morning Gerald's mother and brother came to the hearing. Gerald admitted that he had dialed the telephone when the call had been made. The judge sent him back to the detention home to wait for his next hearing.

Several days later the court told Gerald's mother that the boy's next hearing would be held the following Monday morning. Both of Gerald's parents came to court with Gerald for that hearing. The probation officer had filed papers with specific charges against Gerald. One charge was making nasty remarks to the woman on the phone. No one had told Gerald's family about the charges.

Gerald's mother asked that the woman who accused Gerald appear in court. The judge refused the request. He said that Gerald had already admitted in court that he had spoken during the phone call. Gerald's parents said that Gerald had admitted only to dialing the number.

The probation officer thought that Gerald's parents were right. There were no records of the hearing, though. No one had written down the questions, answers, and comments. The courts usually did not keep such records in cases that involved juveniles.

If an adult had been charged with this crime, the greatest sentence he or she could have gotten would have been a $50 fine or two months in prison. Because Gerald was a juvenile, though, he faced a much stronger sentence.

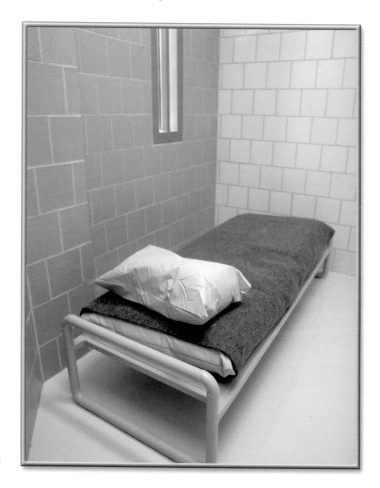

Six Years in Jail!

The court declared Gerald a "**juvenile delinquent**." The judge sent him to Arizona's State Industrial School. Under Arizona law, he was supposed to serve time until he became an adult— at the age of 21!

In the 1960s in Arizona, appeals were not allowed in cases that tried juveniles. However, a special kind of request was made for Gerald. This request was made because Gerald hadn't been given the same rights as adults, even though his punishment was very serious. Lawyers who filed the request made these points:

◆ Gerald and his parents hadn't received notice of the charges against him, so they couldn't prepare for the hearing.

◆ He was sent to the state **reform school** within a week of the crime.

◆ He wasn't told that he could have a lawyer while he was in court.

◀ *Juvenile delinquents are often sent to detention homes with rooms like this one.*

◆ He wasn't given the chance to question the victim or any witnesses.

◆ He wasn't told that he could remain silent or that the things he said could be used against him.

If Gerald had been an adult, he could not have been treated this way. However, the courts did not have to grant juveniles the same rights as adults.

The Gault case changed the rights of juveniles. This case was argued in the U. S. Supreme Court. The court ruled that juveniles charged with a crime should have many of the same basic rights as adults. They should receive notice of charges. They should be told they have the right to an attorney and the right to remain silent. They should have the right to question witnesses.

Where Did the Differences Come From?

Many people were angry about how Gerald had been treated in court. Actually, his treatment might have been a legal accident. Juveniles had not always been treated so harshly in the United States.

In the earliest days of the United States, juveniles were treated the same way as adults were treated. Their cases were heard in the same courts as adult cases. Juveniles could receive the same serious punishments as adults, and they were placed in the same prisons.

Many people thought this approach was wrong. They argued that young people who had committed crimes should be given a chance to change the way they behaved. They could still become strong and helpful members of society.

In the late 1800s, Illinois created the first court for juveniles. Juveniles were sent to reform schools instead of to adult prisons. Soon most other states followed this example. Juveniles were treated less harshly than adults. There were two sets of rules, one for adults and another for juveniles.

In the new system, juveniles would not go through criminal trials, as adults do. Instead, the court would act as a substitute parent for these young people. The law wouldn't state a specific punishment for each crime. The judge would look at each case on its own and decide what should happen to the juvenile.

That's where problems occurred. The two sets of rules usually meant juveniles got easier sentences for crimes. Because they didn't go through actual trials, though, they didn't get the same rights as adults. Without those rights, kids like Gerald Gault could be treated much more harshly than adults. Gault's case went a long way toward giving juveniles the same rights as adults. ⚡

From Juvenile to Adult

When does a person legally become an adult? The age varies from state to state. Once a person reaches that age, he or she faces the law as an adult.

When the accused is a juvenile, the judge decides what punishment is best.

In very serious crimes, a juvenile might stand trial as an adult. This may happen when a crime is particularly violent. In such cases, a judge decides that the juvenile will be treated as an adult before, during, and after the trial.

Juvenile court records are usually sealed to protect a young person's future. That way, people cannot look at those records and hold them against the juvenile later. This gives the juvenile the chance to start life over with a clean record. After all, kids can make poor choices. They also can learn from their mistakes. Because the records are sealed, one early mistake doesn't have to ruin a young person's future.

CHAPTER 6

Victims' Rights

In 1999 a grandmother was riding in a car with her son, her daughter-in-law, two grandchildren, and a friend. They had no idea that in one terrible second their lives would be torn apart.

As they drove along, they were suddenly staring into the headlights of a car coming toward them. That car had a drunk driver at the wheel. They couldn't stop him from slamming into their car.

One drunk driver can hurt many people.

Medical workers rushed to the scene and treated the victims. A rescue helicopter carried the grandmother to a hospital. Doctors managed to save the lives of the accident victims.

That was not the end of the story, though. The grandmother had such serious injuries that she needed many operations. Her son had suffered a severe head wound, and her friend had almost lost an eye. The victims had to live with physical scars and terrifying memories of their **ordeal**.

A year later, the suspect went on trial for the accident. He was found guilty of driving drunk. His lawyer asked the judge to show the man mercy and to have the man's driver's license **suspended** for just one year.

Then something happened that probably wouldn't have been allowed before the 1990s. One of the prosecuting lawyers presented a **victim-impact statement** to the court.

The statement was written by the grandmother who'd been hurt. In it, she told how she and the other victims had suffered from the man's decision to drive drunk. Her statement described the injuries of the other victims. It told about how she had almost died. It told about the surgery on her face and about numerous visits to doctors. It told how she had lived in constant pain since the accident.

The woman was present in the courtroom for the driver's sentencing. Because of her injuries, though, she couldn't read her statement to the court herself. The prosecuting lawyer read it for her.

This victim-impact statement might have helped the court decide on a sentence.

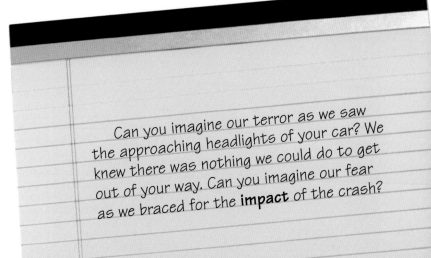

Can you imagine our terror as we saw the approaching headlights of your car? We knew there was nothing we could do to get out of your way. Can you imagine our fear as we braced for the **impact** of the crash?

The judge listened to the victim-impact statement and studied photos of the woman's injuries. Then he made his decision. The driver would not have his license suspended for a year. It would be suspended for 11 years, and the driver would serve seven and one-half years in prison. ⚡

Many people are hurt each year by drunk drivers.

Crimes Have Victims

In recent times more than nine million people have been hurt by violent crimes each year. You've learned about the rights of the accused. Victims have rights, too. For example, victims have the right to ask police officers to investigate crimes. They also have the right to ask that charges be filed against someone who has committed a crime.

The person who committed that crime has many rights. Many people feel that victims need more rights. After all, they've suffered from a crime that someone else committed.

A New Amendment?

In 1982 the state of California passed a victims' rights law, and many other states followed. Some legal experts think that state laws aren't enough, though. They want a new law, the Crime Victims' Rights Amendment, to be added to the United States Constitution.

If passed, the Constitutional amendment will give victims several rights. These rights include:

- *The right to be informed of all court dates in the case and the right to be in court at all times when information about the case is heard.* Crimes can have a big impact on a victim's life. Many victims would like to know exactly what is happening with the case.

- *The right to be heard at important times as the case travels through the legal system.* Victims often feel they have no say in the way a case is handled. For example, sometimes defendants can get a lighter sentence by pleading guilty. Victims would like to have their voices heard in such matters.

- *The right to know if the defendant is released or has escaped.* Many victims of violent crimes fear for their safety when a defendant leaves prison.

◆ *The right to have the case tried quickly.* Many victims are anxious to see justice done. Some court cases can take a long time before they are tried.

◆ *The right to receive money for injuries.* Some victims end up with big medical bills. Others might not be able to work for a while. Defendants sometimes must pay fines if they are found guilty, but this money usually doesn't go to the victim of the crime.

Another Side of the Argument

Not all lawyers support the new amendment, even if they support victims' rights. They believe that some people in the United States could lose rights if the law is passed. For example, victims want the right to demand a speedy trial. If a victim could force a speedy trial, the accused might not have enough time to prepare a defense.

In addition, a single crime might have many victims. What if each one has a different idea about how the case should be settled? Some people argue that the lawyers for the state can decide the best way to handle the case and best serve everyone's interests.

Many victims want the right to be in the courtroom throughout the trial. This is a problem because the victim can also be a witness. In a trial, lawyers often ask that all witnesses be kept out of the courtroom except the witness who is answering questions at that time. Both sides have the legal right to ask for this, and they usually do. That way, one witness can't confuse or influence another witness.

A Balancing Act

Some victims feel that the courts see them only as pieces of evidence, like photographs or fingerprints. Groups that support victims' rights argue that innocent victims should have rights just as guilty criminals do.

It is not easy to decide where to balance the rights of defendants and victims.

Should victims have as many rights as defendants? What happens when a victim's rights conflict with a defendant's rights? There is no clear answer to these questions.

It's important to remember one thing, though. By protecting the rights of the accused, the courts protect the rights of all United States citizens. Anyone can be accused of a crime. Everyone has the right to a fair trial. The cases you've just read about have led to some important rights. These rights help assure that people accused of a crime do get a fair trial.

Glossary

accused (uh KYOOZD) *noun* The accused is the person who is charged with a crime.

amendments (uh MEHND muhnts) *noun* Amendments are changes or additions to the U. S. Constitution.

appoint (uh POYNT) *verb* To appoint means to name someone to do something.

bumper (BUHM puhr) *noun* A bumper is a metal or rubber bar attached to the front and back of a car to protect it in a crash.

burglary (BUR gluh ree) *adjective* A burglary scene is a place where someone entered a building to steal something.

clients (KLY uhnts) *noun* Clients are a lawyer's customers.

committed (kuh MIHT ihd) *verb* Someone who committed a crime did something that was against the law.

competent (KAHM puh tuhnt) *adjective* When a person is competent, he or she can understand charges and can help the lawyer prepare a case.

confession (kuhn FEHSH uhn) *noun* A confession is a statement of guilt that someone makes.

convict (kuhn VIHKT) *verb* To convict means to find someone guilty of a crime.

conviction (kuhn VIHK shuhn) *noun* A conviction is the judgment by a judge or jury that a person is guilty as charged.

cross-examination (KRAWS ehg zam uh NAY shuhn) *noun* Cross-examination is the act of a lawyer questioning the witnesses called by the opposite side.

defendant (dee FEHN duhnt) *noun* A defendant is a person against whom charges are filed.

detention home (dee TEHN shuhn HOHM) *noun* A detention home is a place where young people are held after they've committed crimes.

direct examination (duh REHKT ehg zam uh NAY shuhn) *noun* Direct examination is the act of a lawyer questioning witnesses called by his or her own side.

guarantee (gar uhn TEE) *verb* To guarantee means to promise or make certain of something.

impact (IHM pakt) *noun* An impact is an effect or a change produced by being touched or moved.

imprint (IHM prihnt) *adjective* Imprint means related to a mark or pattern made by something pressing on a surface.

improper (ihm PRAHP uhr) *adjective* An action is improper when it offends people or breaks accepted rules.

insanity (ihn SAN uh tee) *noun* Insanity is a state of mind in which a person doesn't know right from wrong or can't control himself or herself.

jury (JUR ee) *noun* A jury is a group of people who make a decision in a court case.

juvenile delinquent (JOO vuh nyl dih LIHNG kwuhnt) *noun* A juvenile delinquent is a young person who breaks the law.

juveniles (JOO vuh nylz) *noun* Juveniles are young people.

lineup (LYN uhp) *noun* A lineup is a group of people that includes a suspect. Police ask a victim to identify the person who committed the crime.

mental (MEHNT uhl) *adjective* Mental means related to the mind.

ordeal (awr DEEL) *noun* An ordeal is a difficult experience.

probation (proh BAY shuhn) *adjective* Probation means related to a sentence that requires a person to meet certain demands of the court, such as working in the community, instead of going to jail.

prosecuting lawyer (PRAHS uh kyoot ihng LAW yuhr) *noun* A prosecuting lawyer is a lawyer who tries to prove that a person is guilty of a crime.

reform school (rih FAWRM SKOOL) *noun* A reform school is a place to which juvenile delinquents are sent instead of prison.

saliva (suh LY vuh) *noun* Saliva, or spit, is a mixture of fluids in the mouth.

self-defense (SEHLF dih FEHNS) *noun* Self-defense is the act of protecting oneself in an attack.

suspended (suh SPEHN dihd) *adjective* Suspended means stopped for a period of time.

teller (TEHL uhr) *adjective* A teller machine (ATM) handles money.

testify (TEHS tuh fy) *verb* To testify is to be a witness or to speak in court.

tried (TRYD) *adjective* Tried means put on trial in a court of law.

unreasonable (uhn REE zuhn uh buhl) *adjective* Unreasonable means beyond reason or having no reason.

verdict (VUR dihkt) *noun* A verdict is a decision of guilty or not guilty in a court case.

victim-impact statement (VIHK tuhm IHM pakt STAYT muhnt) *noun* A victim-impact statement is a statement by the victim of a crime. It describes how the crime has affected his or her life.

violated (VY uh layt ihd) *verb* Violated means failed to keep, or broke.

wallets (WAH lihts) *noun* Wallets are carrying cases for money and credit cards.

Index